How To...

INCLUDES ONLINE VIDEO LESSONS WITH DEMONSTRATIONS
OF ALL THE PLAYING EXAMPLES IN THE BOOK

FINGERPICK SONGS ON GUITAR

ESSENTIAL PATTERNS, TECHNIQUES & ARRANGING CONCEPTS

BY CHAD JOHNSON

To access video visit:
www.halleonard.com/mylibrary

Enter Code
5563-5612-1672-0377

ISBN 978-1-4950-5635-2

HAL•LEONARD®

7777 W. BLUEMOUND RD. P.O. BOX 13819 MILWAUKEE, WI 53213

In Australia Contact:
Hal Leonard Australia Pty. Ltd.
4 Lentara Court
Cheltenham, Victoria, 3192 Australia
Email: ausadmin@halleonard.com.au

Visit Hal Leonard Online at
www.halleonard.com

CONTENTS

ABOUT THE AUTHOR

Chad Johnson is a freelance author, editor, and musician. For Hal Leonard Corporation, he has authored over 70 instructional books covering a variety of instruments and topics, including *Guitarist's Guide to Scales Over Chords*, *The Hal Leonard Fingerstyle Guitar Method*, *How to Record at Home on a Budget*, *Teach Yourself to Play Bass Guitar*, *Ukulele Aerobics*, *Pentatonic Scales for Guitar: The Essential Guide*, *Pink Floyd Guitar Signature Licks*, and *Play Like Robben Ford*, to name but a few. He's a featured instructor on the DVD *200 Country Guitar Licks* (also published by Hal Leonard) and has toured and performed throughout the East Coast in various bands, sharing the stage with members of Lynyrd Skynyrd, the Allman Brothers Band, Jamey Johnson, and others. He works as a session instrumentalist, composer/songwriter, and recording engineer when not authoring or editing and currently resides in Denton, TX (North Dallas) with his wife and two children. Feel free to contact him at chadjohnsonguitar@gmail.com with any questions or concerns and follow him at www.facebook.com/chadjohnsonguitar.

INTRODUCTION

Welcome to *How to Fingerpick Songs on Guitar*. In this book, we're going to look at beginning fingerstyle techniques and how they can be used to play great-sounding arrangements of your favorite songs. If you're completely new to the world of fingerstyle guitar, you're in the right place. We pretty much start at ground zero here with regard to technique. However, if you've already got a handle on the basics, don't dismay; there's still plenty for you as well.

Fingerstyle technique opens up entire new worlds of expression on the guitar. Not only is the tone different than when using a pick, but you suddenly have access to rhythmic, harmonic, and melodic sophistication that pick-only players can only dream of. Although we don't have the complete bass/melody independence of the piano, for example, we can get pretty darn close with practice. Fingerstyle guitar is also arguably the most intimate, hands-on connection you can have with the instrument, which feels rewarding on its own.

This book will focus on the acoustic guitar, but just about any of the concepts taught within can be transferred to the electric as well. The string spacing may be a little narrower on an electric guitar, but you should be able to adjust to that fairly quickly. So, if you don't own an acoustic yet, feel free to begin the lessons with an electric. When you do go shopping for an acoustic guitar, keep in mind that, if you do want to use it primarily for fingerstyle playing, then you should try it out that way. In other words, if all you can do is strum some chords right now, but you really want an acoustic guitar that sounds especially nice with fingerpicking, try to find someone accomplished in that style and see if they wouldn't mind playing several different models for you to help make your decision.

Without further ado, let's get started. Welcome to the world of fingerpicking!

HOW TO USE THIS BOOK

This book assumes that you already have some background on the guitar, such as strumming chords and/or playing some lead, so it's not an absolute beginner's method. However, it does pretty much start from scratch with regard to fingerstyle technique, so no player should be left behind. Although the book does cover several different fingerstyle techniques (arpeggiation, block chords, etc.), it should not be thought of as a reference book. For best results—especially if you're a beginner—it should be worked through in a comprehensive manner, from front to back. Even if you have some experience with fingerpicking, please work through the earlier examples at least once, as there may be some terminology or concepts with which you're unfamiliar.

We begin by introducing basic fingerpicking techniques to get you comfortable with the idea. These techniques will be demonstrated with exercises and examples in various styles. In the second half of the book, we'll look at how these concepts can be used to play solo-style arrangements of several songs. The introductory techniques taught in the first several chapters all play a part in the solo arrangements, so they need to be mastered before attempting the latter chapters. By the time you're through, you'll be armed with several great-sounding arrangements with which to impress your friends, family, pets, etc. We'll even discuss the process involved in creating your own arrangements. Proceed with this material at your own pace. If you have trouble understanding any concept, be sure to check out the accompanying videos, as they will likely shed some light on the topic.

ABOUT THE VIDEO

Each chapter in the book includes a full video lesson, so you can see and hear the material being taught. To access all of the videos that accompany this book, simply go to **www.halleonard.com/ mylibrary** and enter the code found on page 1. The music examples that include video are marked with an icon throughout the book, and the timecode listed with each icon tells you exactly where on the video the example is performed.

I should mention that some fingerstyle players prefer to use a thumbpick. Mr. Guitar himself, Chet Atkins, preferred this approach, as does Nashville super-picker Brent Mason. If you're completely new to fingerpicking, you might want to try one to see how it feels. Other players, such as Paul Simon and James Taylor, go without. Compared to the thumb alone, the thumbpick will generally provide a bit of a crisper sound (depending on how much nail is used when plucking with the thumb) and the opportunity to switch to a flatpick style, as Brent Mason is known to do.

By the same token, some people prefer to grow their nails out a bit and pluck the strings with them (classical players do this, for instance), while others prefer to use their flesh. Nails will sound brighter and more brilliant, whereas flesh will sound darker and perhaps more "earthy." Again, the choice is yours. If players play exclusively with their nails, they'll often take care of them by filing them in a particular way and/or applying nail strengthener to harden them. If you're interested, you can find a great deal of information about nail maintenance online.

Also realize that, if you're completely new to fingerpicking, your plucking-hand finger tips are most likely going to get sore at first—just as your fret-hand fingers did when you first started playing. This is normal and will subside once you begin to build up your callouses. So take it easy at first and don't overdo it. As is always the case with any instrument, it's better to practice for 30 minutes or an hour every day than six hours straight on Saturday only!

CHAPTER 1

BASIC TECHNIQUE ▶

When fingerpicking on the guitar, different people use different combinations of plucking-hand fingers, depending on the style being played. Classical players mostly use their thumb, index, middle, and ring fingers (although flamenco style employs the pinky on occasion as well), but many folk and country players often use only the thumb, index, and middle. Still other players, such as the late Merle Travis and Sir Paul McCartney, predominantly use only the thumb and index finger or, in the case of country virtuoso Jerry Reed, the thumb and middle finger.

If you're just starting out, I'd suggest adopting a thumb, index, middle, and ring approach, as it will afford you the most versatility. We label the fingers of the plucking hand in the music with names derived from Spanish:

- thumb = *p* (pulgar)

- index = *i* (indice)

- middle = *m* (medio)

- ring = *a* (anular)

- pinky = *c* (chiquito)

(Again, the pinky is rarely used outside of flamenco and some jazz styles, and we won't be using it in this book.)

PLACING THE FINGERS

To begin, plant your thumb on string 6, index finger on string 3, middle finger on string 2, and ring finger on string 1. Your thumb should be farther up the string (toward the neck) than your index finger by an inch or so, depending on the size of your hand. If you arch your wrist out a bit from the guitar, when you look down, you should see a small triangle created by the thumb, index finger, and the string:

Having the wrist nice and arched like this is the classical position, but the majority of non-classical players don't go to this extreme; they usually collapse the wrist a bit and use a position closer to that of pick style, like this:

While working on the early exercises in this book, you should experiment with your hand placement to find a position that's comfortable for you. Depending on the shape and size of your hands, it will vary from one person to the next, but I will caution you: avoid anything too extreme (i.e., severely arched or bent in another way that causes strain in any part of your arm or wrist).

GAINING FAMILIARITY

With your hand in position and thumb/fingers planted on strings 6, 3, 2, and 1, experiment with different amounts of weight on the strings. Press in on the strings a bit and then ease up again. Remove them completely and then replant them. Just get used to the feeling of having your fingers planted and ready to go. When you start to feel comfortable with that, it's time to play our first exercise.

We're going to use open strings to play an arpeggio here. An *arpeggio* is simply the notes of a chord played one at a time instead of all together. The open strings that we're using (6, 3, 2, and 1) are a nice place to start because they happen to form an E minor chord. Pluck *p–i–m–a* in quarter notes, letting the notes ring together throughout the measure. When you reach the end of the measure, replant all four digits and repeat the exercise. This means that you'll be stopping (muting) all four strings every time you start.

When plucking with your thumb, make sure that you're plucking with the entire thumb and not just bending the knuckle. Using the knuckle results in a weaker, inferior tone that's harder to control. You want to keep the thumb fairly straight while plucking so that the motion comes from the hand/thumb joint.

Let's try the reverse of our first example; this time, we'll pluck *a–m–i–p*. Again, replant all four fingers before beat 1 each time.

EXERCISE 1 ▶ • 1:23

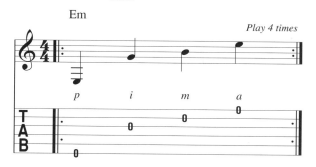

EXERCISE 2 ▶ • 2:02

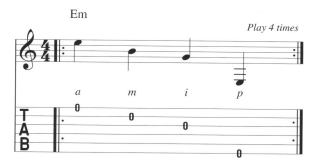

TECHNICAL TALK

When plucking with the thumb, there are two main options for plucking the string: the free stroke and the rest stroke. Even though you weren't aware of it, you were most likely doing one of the two. With a *free stroke*, your thumb is not touching any strings after you pluck. With a *rest stroke*, your thumb comes to rest on the adjacent string after plucking. So, after you pluck string 6, for example, the thumb will come to rest on string 5.

Generally, rest strokes provide a louder, fuller tone because you're plucking down into the guitar, which results in greater string resonance. However, rest strokes can't always be used because you may be muting a string that you want to ring out. I tend to use rest strokes when possible (not always) and switch to free stroke when muting is a concern. I encourage you to practice both methods and note the difference in feel and tone.

It should be mentioned that the same two strokes apply to the fingers, as well, although rest strokes with the fingers are generally applied to playing single-note lines because, again, you would end up muting a lot of notes if you used rest strokes consistently.

Let's try playing the same ascending arpeggio pattern but adding a chord change, as well. We'll move from Em to G, which only requires adding two fretted notes.

EXERCISE 3  • 3:53

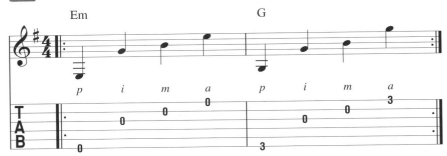

And now we'll go up the Em chord and down the G chord. This means that we'll be playing the ring finger and the thumb twice in a row. This is no cause for alarm; simply take your time and remember to replant all the fingers before plucking again.

EXERCISE 4  • 4:29

Let's move on to some other strings now. In a very general sense, you could say that the thumb often handles strings 6–4 and the fingers handle strings 3–1. However, there are many exceptions to this, so it shouldn't be considered a rule in any sense. Let's demonstrate this fact right now by working with C and Am chords. We'll play on strings 5–2 here, with our thumb handling string 5 and the other fingers falling into place.

EXERCISE 5  • 5:21

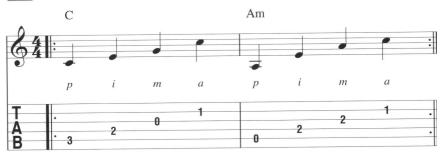

EXERCISE 6  • 5:48

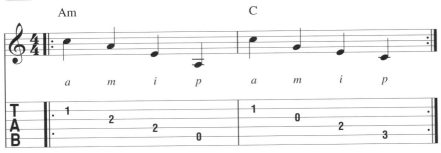

CHAPTER 2
EASY ARPEGGIOS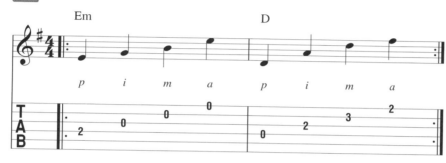

Now that you're familiar with the concept of fingerpicking arpeggios, we'll explore them more thoroughly in this chapter. There are an almost limitless number of patterns that you can create by combining, varying, or expanding upon more basic ones, and many artists have done just that when creating timeless fingerpicking riffs.

Let's expand our repertoire with several examples that use different chords and arpeggio patterns. We're still playing only one note at a time here, but we'll mix up the order of the notes a bit more in this chapter. Let's begin by working with the 4–1 string group, with our thumb assigned to string 4. However, as opposed to the last chapter, don't replant your fingers on the strings when you repeat this time. In other words, allow all the strings to ring out continuously.

EXERCISE 1  • 0:43

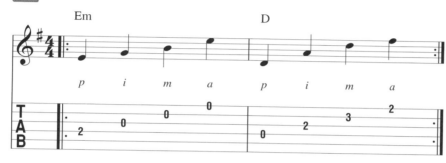

EXERCISE 2  • 1:37

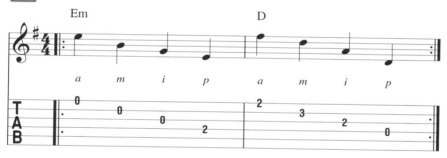

Replanting all the fingers at once, as we did in Chapter 1, is a great way to get a feel for the technique, but it's imperative that you learn to operate both ways. In some instances, replanting will be necessary to prevent an unwanted note or two from ringing, while other times, when the ringing notes from chord to chord sound good, it can rob a pattern's musical flow. I'd suggest getting used to both methods early on and trying the remaining arpeggio examples in the book with each one.

THINKING AHEAD

Exercises 1 and 2 are great demonstrations of another important concept to consider early on in your development: continuity. Many times, certain concessions need to be made in order for a fingerpicking pattern to sound smooth. One of these is *alternate fingerings*.

Consider Exercise 1 for a second: When moving from D back to Em, most people would likely choose either the first, second, or perhaps the third finger (if they were fretting a full, six-string Em chord with the middle and ring fingers) of the left hand for the E note on string 4. Assuming you're playing the D chord with the usual fingering—index, ring, and middle on strings 3, 2, and 1, respectively—then you wouldn't want to use the middle finger for the Em chord because it's fretting the last note of the D chord. Bringing it down to string 4 will inevitably clip that last note short just a bit. With practice, you can move very quickly and make the gap less noticeable. The better method, however, is to simply use the first finger for the E note on string 4. That way, you can time the release of the middle finger (from the F# note on string 1) with the striking of the first note in the Em chord, thereby making the transition perfectly smooth.

Another similar concept is *common tones*. This idea is perfectly demonstrated in Exercises 5 and 6 from Chapter 1. When moving from C to Am (or vice versa), there's no need to lift your first or second fingers because they're common to both chords. Leaving them fretted will ensure a smooth transition from chord to chord. It's good to get into this habit early on (i.e., examining your fingering choices and looking for opportunities to smooth things out).

Let's try an example now in which we shift our right-hand thumb to different strings for the bass notes. For the Cmaj7 chord, the thumb will play string 5, but for G, it will play string 6. The fret hand's job here is very easy: playing only one note for each chord. Make sure to allow the open strings to ring out continuously for maximum effect. We're playing eighth notes now, but the tempo is slow, so it's not that much faster than the previous examples. Exercise 4 is similar to 3, but the order of the treble notes has been reversed.

Here's a variation on the alternating-thumb idea, this time with Am and E chords. In these examples, our fingers are playing strings 4–2, though. When playing the low E string at the beginning of the E chord, be sure to use a rest stroke. Why? Because we don't want the open A string ringing out during the E chord, and using a rest stroke on string 6 means that the thumb will come to rest on string 5 and stop it. The open E string ringing through the Am chord isn't as problematic because that note (E) is contained in the Am chord, as well. However, if you'd like to stop it, you can do so by lightly touching it with your fret-hand thumb over the top of the neck.

We'll switch to a 12/8 time signature here, which we'll basically feel as four beats of triplets. When moving from Fmaj7 to C, be sure to notice the common tone between the chords: the C note on string 2. Keep that note fretted throughout!

EXERCISE 7  • 6:14

We're reversing the order of the treble notes here:

EXERCISE 8 • 6:45

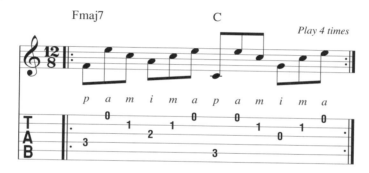

Now let's check out some examples in various styles. Here's a 12/8 riff that sounds great with rolling arpeggios. We'll use the six-note *p–i–m–a–m–i* pattern for most of the chords here but we'll mix it up a little in some spots for variation.

FINGERPICKING RIFF 1 • 7:17

In this next example, which is in a Jimmy Page vein, we're sticking mostly to an ascending *p–i–m–a* pattern, with the thumb and fingers assigned to strings 5–2 in measure 1. From then on, however, your fingers remain assigned to strings 4–2, and your thumb shifts to string 6 and stays there. The fret hand does have a bit of work to do here, so take some time to familiarize yourself with the chord shapes and be sure to take advantage of the common tones! For the final Am chord, just brush through the strings with your thumb.

FINGERPICKING RIFF 2 ▶ • 8:47

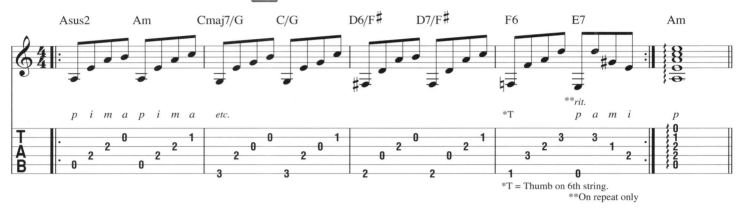

TECHNIQUE REMINDER

Are you remembering your common tones? Be sure not to lift the D note when moving from F6 to E7 in Fingerpicking Riff 2. It's a little thing, but it makes quite a noticeable difference!

This next riff is reminiscent of Bon Jovi's Richie Sambora and mixes a droning open D string with ascending 6th intervals from the D Dorian mode on strings 3 and 1. We're using a *p–i–a–i* pattern here exclusively.

FINGERPICKING RIFF 3 ▶ • 9:33

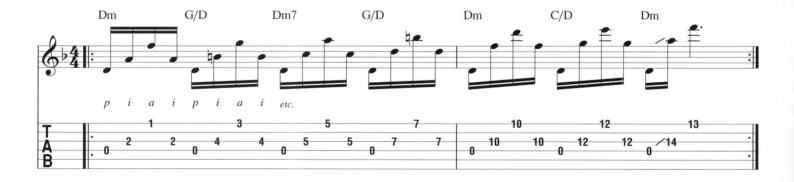

CHAPTER 3
PINCHING (PLAYING TWO NOTES AT ONCE) ▶

Now that you've gotten the hang of basic arpeggios, it's time to step it up a bit with a technique called *pinching*. This refers to playing two notes (one with the thumb and one with a finger) at once. There isn't much new in the way of technique, but it may take a bit of practice to synchronize the attacks of the thumb and finger. Pinching is an essential technique to master, however, because it really allows you to start playing more melodically.

Let's try it out with a simple C–Am progression. Plant your thumb and fingers on strings 5–2 and leave them there throughout. On beats 1 and 3, pinch strings 5 and 2 with your thumb and ring finger, respectively, continuing with *m* and *i*.

EXERCISE 1 ▶ • 0:26

Here's an exercise that really isolates the technique. This time, we're pinching with the thumb and middle finger. You'll see this exact type of move in lots of fingerstyle songs.

EXERCISE 2 ▶ • 1:11

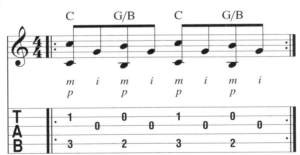

This next example pushes the envelope a bit further. We're playing a descending finger pattern on the C chord and then switching to an ascending pattern on the F chord. This means that we're pinching the *p* and *a* on the C chord and *p* and *i* on the F chord. We're also shifting string groups from 5–2 to 4–1, so take it slowly. This is a good time to bring up another fingering strategy for smooth chord transitions: *partial fretting*. If it's difficult for you to fret the Cadd9 chord all at once after the Fm chord, note that you don't have to. You only need to fret strings 5 and 2 on the downbeat (the E note on string 4 doesn't need to be fretted right away).

EXERCISE 3 ▶ • 2:51

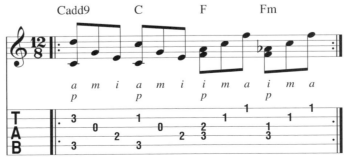

Let's continue on with some other examples that demonstrate the possibilities of this technique. This one is in D minor and uses a similar concept to Fingerpicking Riff 3 from Chapter 2: moving triads over a static open D bass note. This one is in 3/4 time.

EXERCISE 4  • 3:16

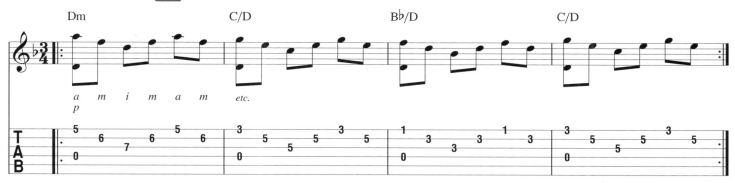

Here's a pretty one in E major that simply walks the same form up to different diatonic harmonies. We remain on string group 4–1 throughout, so it's relatively easy for the plucking hand. Be sure to take advantage of the open B string at the end of beat 2, measure 1 when shifting up to the G♯m chord.

EXERCISE 5 • 4:20

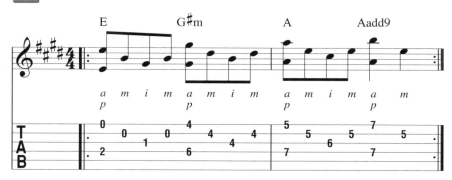

We're beginning to get a bit more independence between bass and treble parts in this next example. The bass notes (thumb) are only played on beats 1 and 3, but the melody on string 2 is syncopated a bit. Keep your thumb and fingers planted on strings 6 and 4–2, respectively. (Later on, we'll learn an alternate way to pluck this type of figure.)

EXERCISE 6 • 5:17

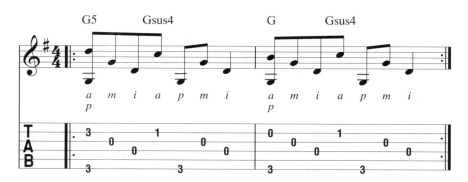

Next we have a typical application of the idea from Exercise 2. We're moving between C and Am chords, with the G/B acting as a passing chord. Your plucking hand will remain on the 5–2 string group throughout.

EXERCISE 7 ▶ • 6:21

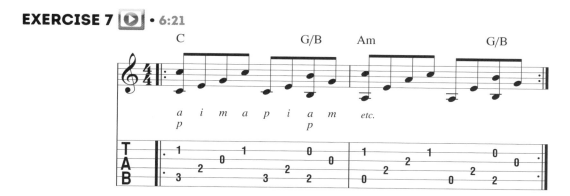

Now let's check out the pinching technique in a few riffs. Here's a classic application of the idea, with a few bass notes added beneath a rolling arpeggio pattern on the high strings consisting of melody notes on string 1 and open droning strings 2 and 3. Keep your *i*, *m*, and *a* fingers assigned to strings 3, 2, and 1, respectively, throughout. Your thumb remains on string 6. As such, try using a rest stroke with the thumb for a more powerful bass line.

FINGERPICKING RIFF 1 ▶ • 6:57

Here's another take on the droning open D string idea with various triads moving above it. This time, we're playing descending three-note arpeggios—again, from the D Dorian mode—with an *a–m–i* pattern against the thumb-plucked D string. I use the index finger of the fret hand for all the notes on string 1, including some half barres, to maintain fluidity throughout.

FINGERPICKING RIFF 2 ▶ • 8:07

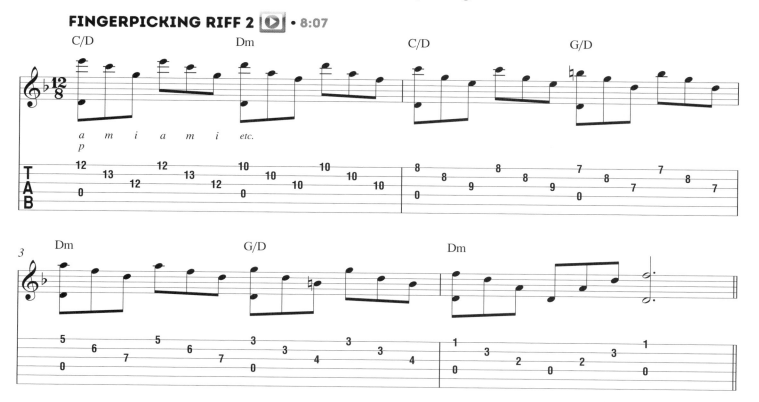

We'll close this chapter with another riff in D minor—this time, in 3/4 meter and in the style of Jim Croce. This is the most difficult example thus far, as it features challenges to both hands. The plucking hand is straightforward in the beginning, with a rolling *a–m–i* pattern coupled with *p* strokes on the downbeats, but in measure 5, the pattern begins to alternate, so keep an eye out for that. The fretting hand includes some stretches and finger-twisting chords that will require a good look before tackling the whole example. "Economy of motion" is crucial here, as is maintaining common tones between chords when possible. Check out the video to see how I finger this one.

FINGERPICKING RIFF 3 ▶ • 9:41

CHAPTER 4

BLOCK-CHORD STYLE

While arpeggiation is playing a chord one note at a time, *block-chord style* involves using three or four digits to pluck a whole chord at once. This is reminiscent of piano players, as they often attack notes in this fashion.

As with pinching two notes, the issue of making the attacks uniform and simultaneous arises. In this regard, many players actually keep their *i*, *m*, and *a* fingers in contact with one another, almost as if they were glued together. This can help them perform as one single unit, ensuring that all the strings are attacked at the same time.

Let's try a few simple exercises to get a feel for the technique. For this first example, your fingers will remain on strings 4–2 while your thumb moves from string 5 to string 6 and back. Try to produce an even volume throughout so that each note can be heard.

EXERCISE 1  • 0:51

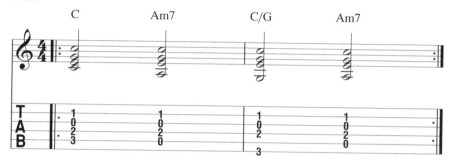

We'll mix in some quarter notes here. If you've been practicing your replanting with the previous examples in the book, this should be easier for you.

EXERCISE 2  • 1:17

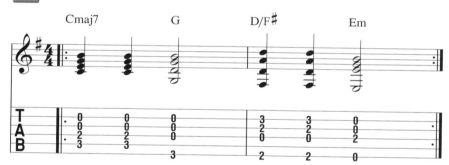

We move through several chords on top of an A pedal in the bass here. Watch out for the string group shift on beat 4 of measure 1!

EXERCISE 3 • 1:57

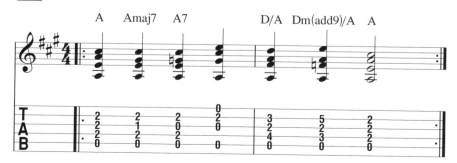

BLOCK-CHORD VARIATIONS

It's actually somewhat rare that a player will play chords like this exclusively. More often than not, they'll use a slight variation in which the bass note and the fingers separate at times and play together at others (again, similar to a piano player).

For example, instead of playing something like this, which is a cool-sounding syncopated groove in E:

EXERCISE 4A  • 2:35

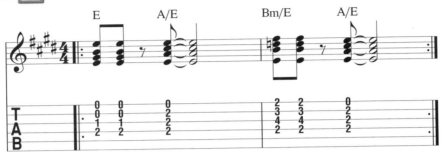

You can separate the thumb and fingers at times to get something like this:

EXERCISE 4B • 2:57

Many times, this idea can feel more natural than playing all four notes together every time, but if it's awkward at first, be sure to slow the tempo down until you get it.

Here's an example in A minor. Notice that, although the fingers are playing a syncopated rhythm, the thumb is only playing on beats 1 and 3. Also, this is the first example in which the notation shows two separate voices: bass and treble. Whenever you see this, it almost always indicates that the downstemmed notes are played with the thumb and the upstemmed notes are played with the fingers, as is the case here. This separation is usually done on an as-needed basis. If the music is clear when written in one voice, there's no need to use two.

EXERCISE 5 • 3:27

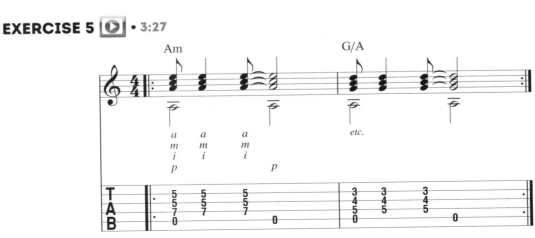

Let's check out a few more possibilities. Another idea is to completely separate the thumb and fingers. In other words, play a bass note and then follow it with some chords. Here's an example of that idea in G. Again, the thumb is only playing on beats 1 and 3.

EXERCISE 6  • 3:50

And here's a nice riff in D that uses a shuffle feel. The thumb is more active here, playing on beats 1, 3, and 4 of each measure. Again, the thumb plays all the downstemmed notes.

EXERCISE 7  • 4:22

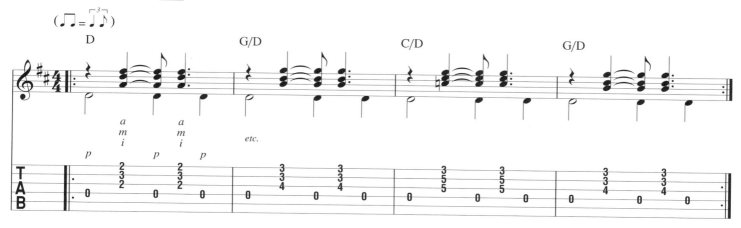

We'll up the ante here by adding a bit of melody to the proceedings. After plucking chords on the downbeat with the fingers and bass notes on the upbeats with the thumb, we play an ascending melody with the thumb to transition to a higher pair of voicings in measure 3. At this point, the roles are reversed: the thumb plays on the downbeats and the fingers play on the upbeats. It wraps up with the fingers playing a descending melody to reconnect with the lower position. Notice the plucking-hand fingerings for the treble melody at the end. The tempo here is slow enough that you could easily use the *m* finger for both notes on string 2, but it's a good idea to get used to alternating fingers when playing single-note melodies like this. At faster tempos, you won't be able to keep up by using only one finger. This type of melody playing is getting closer to an actual solo-guitar arrangement.

EXERCISE 8 • 5:03

Now let's check out how the block-chord technique can be used in some typical riffs. This example uses the separate bass and fingers approach, along with some bass-note movement, to sound a chord progression in G major similar to what Paul McCartney might do. When moving from the G5 chord to the B7 chord, use fingers 2, 3, and 4 for the G5. This way, you can use the pinky as a guide finger when moving to the B7, since it will remain on string 1.

FINGERPICKING RIFF 1 ▶ • 5:44

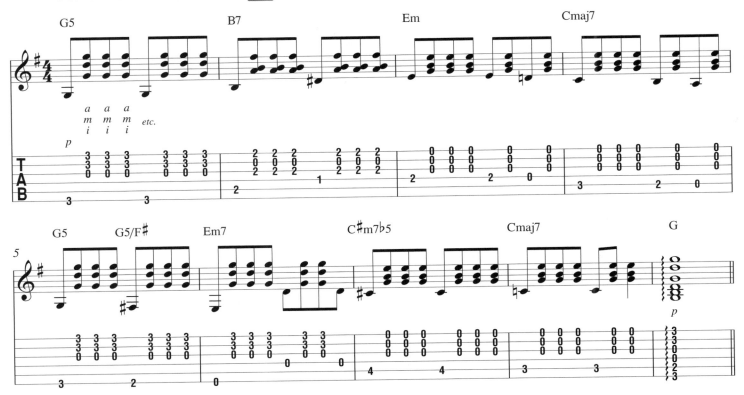

Eric Clapton often uses a block-chord style in which he mostly alternates chords (downbeats) and bass notes (upbeats). This creates a nice, even rhythm that walks steadily through the chords. This riff in A major features a descending bass line, which is a common device in fingerstyle guitar.

FINGERPICKING RIFF 2 ▶ • 6:28

A common variation on the block-chord style is one that simulates a "one-man band" by way of added percussive elements. In this technique, you forcefully plant your plucking-hand fingers on beats 2 and 4 to create a drum-like sound that's reminiscent of a snare. The bass notes and chords are usually separated into two parts and follow a repetitive rhythm, as is the case here. In this riff, the fingers remain on strings 3–1, and the thumb plays all the notes on strings 6, 5, and 4.

FINGERPICKING RIFF 3 ▶ • 7:25

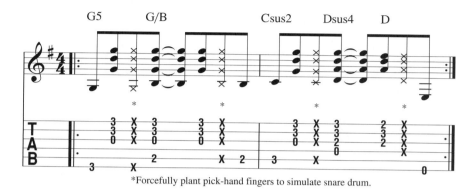

*Forcefully plant pick-hand fingers to simulate snare drum.

Tracy Chapman uses variations on the block-chord style in some of her compositions. This riff hints at that with an ornamental pull-off and some colorful voicings. Notice the downstemmed notes, which should be played by the thumb.

FINGERPICKING RIFF 4 ▶ • 7:55

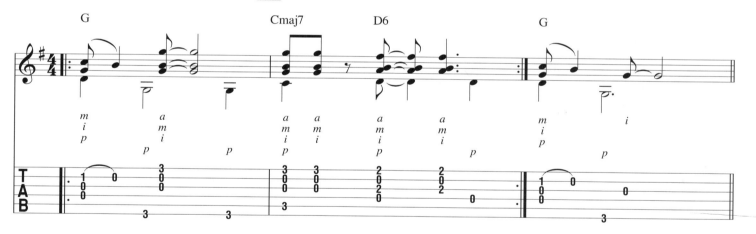

CHAPTER 5
TRAVIS PICKING

One of the most common fingerpicking styles of all has come to be known as *Travis picking*, named after country legend Merle Travis. A pioneer on the instrument, Travis became known for his ability to combine two separate elements—an alternating bass and melodies or chords on top—into one guitar part. Although he actually only used his thumb (a thumbpick actually) and index finger, his style was imitated by others using more digits. Chet Atkins, who used a thumbpick and two fingers (index and middle), became one of the most well-known masters of Travis picking.

Nowadays, the term has been applied to any number of variations in which the thumb is alternating bass notes while the fingers are playing on top—either simultaneously with the thumb or filling in the gaps. The majority of players these days use the thumb, index, and middle fingers when Travis picking, but the ring finger can certainly be used, as well.

Let's take a look at the basic idea. We'll work with the open C chord to start with. First, plant your thumb on string 5, your index on string 3, and your middle on string 2. Then, work on alternately plucking strings 5 and 4 with your thumb, like this:

EXERCISE 1 ▶ • 1:28

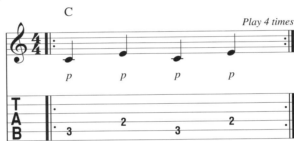

Start slowly at first and make sure that you have this down before proceeding. This is absolutely the backbone of the Travis picking technique. Your thumb is the relentless timekeeper and needs to be as solid as the Rock of Gibraltar! When you start getting into faster tempos (and Travis picking can get *very* fast), the thumb will be on total autopilot while holding down the fort.

So, now that you've gotten the alternating bass feeling steady, try adding the fingers. We're simply going to play in the gaps here (i.e., the upbeats) with our index and middle fingers on strings 3 and 2, respectively. Start as slowly as you need to and work it up to speed once it's comfortable.

EXERCISE 2 ▶ • 2:01

Bam! You're Travis picking! There are almost countless variations on this basic idea. You can vary the order of the treble notes, move them to different strings, add the ring finger, add some pinching, etc. The list goes on and on. But the common thread throughout them all is the alternating bass. This, too, has variation possibilities. Depending on the chord you're playing, you may be alternating between strings 5 and 4, 6 and 4, 5 and 3, 4 and 3, etc.

For example, let's look at a common Travis-picking pattern for a G chord. We're still keeping our index and middle fingers on strings 3 and 2, respectively, but the thumb is now alternating between strings 6 and 4. Practice this motion first, as it will take a bit of getting used to.

EXERCISE 3  • 2:31

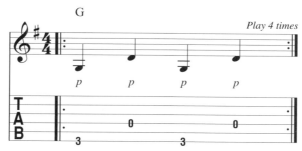

When you've got a good feel for that, add in the fingers to complete the pattern.

EXERCISE 4 • 2:52

Now let's try playing through some short progressions using both types of thumb alternations. First, we'll move from C to Am, with the thumb alternating between strings 5 and 4. It's important to remember your fretting-hand strategies for smooth chord transitions, especially when Travis picking. Also remember the common tones in the fretting hand between C and Am. If you keep them fretted throughout, the riff will sound smooth as silk. Watch the video for a demonstration of how choppy it can sound if you don't do this!

EXERCISE 5 • 4:03

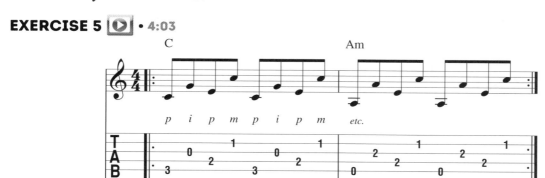

And now we'll move from G to Em, so the thumb will be alternating between strings 6 and 4. Again, the fingers remain on strings 3 and 2.

EXERCISE 6 • 4:27

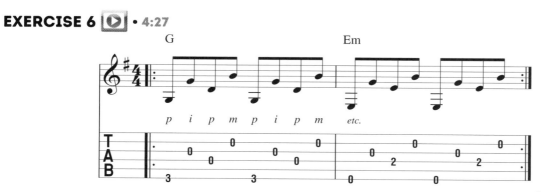

Now let's look at a few more variations. In this example, we're simply reversing the order of the fingers, so the pattern becomes *p–m–p–i*.

EXERCISE 7  • 5:15

In the next exercise, we'll move everything over a string group so that our thumb will alternate between strings 4 and 3, and our index and middle fingers will be assigned to strings 2 and 1, respectively. We've dressed up the E chord in measure 2 with an added 9th on top, as well. Be sure to take advantage of the open E string when shifting up to second position midway through measure 1.

EXERCISE 8 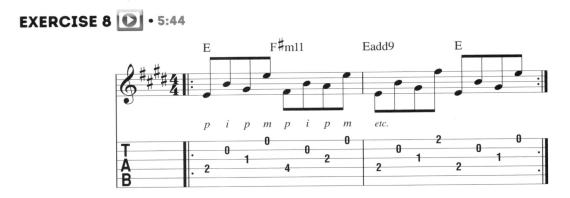 • 5:44

In this one, you'll get some good thumb practice. For the A chord, you'll alternate between strings 5 and 4, but for the E chord, it'll be strings 6 and 4. Be sure not to cut off the last C♯ note (fret 2, string 2) in the A chord when moving to the E chord. Since you're only plucking the open low E string on the downbeat of measure 2, you can leave that C♯ note fretted right up until the E string is plucked and still have time to fret the E chord.

EXERCISE 9  • 6:51

Now let's add a pinch to the pattern. We'll start with our C chord again, but this time the middle finger will pluck on beat 1 with the thumb. Everything else is the same as measure 1 in Exercise 7.

EXERCISE 10 ▶ • 7:32

Now let's bring the ring finger in for some variety. Some players would choose to play this with only two fingers, moving the middle finger over to string 1 and back again, but if you can use your ring finger, why not?

EXERCISE 11 ▶ • 8:04

With a little tweaking of the fingers, we can create a nice ragtime-style riff in G. We're using a shuffle feel and a new pattern in the fingers here. Notice also that we're just playing a quarter-note thumb pluck on beat 4. This omission (the "and" of beat 4) is another very common variation on the Travis-picking style—especially at very fast tempos. Take it slowly and get the pattern cemented in your fingers before speeding it up. Your thumb should start feeling a bit automatic at this point. Notice that you can leave your fret-hand pinky on the B♭ note (fret 3, string 3) throughout the riff.

EXERCISE 12 ▶ • 8:40

There are lots of songs that use Travis picking and variations thereof. Lindsey Buckingham often created beautiful patterns for many of Fleetwood Mac's hits. This riff, reminiscent of the Buckingham style, Travis picks through a cycling IV–I–ii–I progression in which the I chord is in first inversion. This creates stepwise motion in the bass. Notice the capo on fret 2, which puts this song in the key of A instead of G (the key in which it's notated). We're using all three fingers (*i*, *m*, and *a*) on the IV and ii chords but only *i* and *m* on the I chord. This type of variation can help keep patterns from sounding too predictable.

FINGERPICKING RIFF 1 ▶ • 9:44

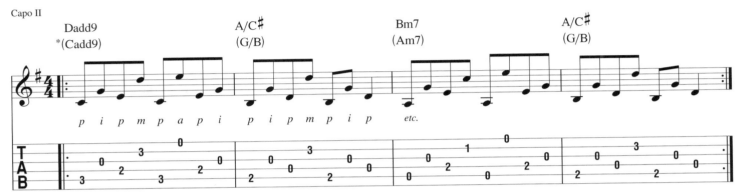

*Symbols in parentheses represent chord names respective to capoed guitar.
Symbols above reflect actual sounding chords. Capoed fret is "0" in tab.

The open G chord is often ornamented in Travis-picking patterns with a C/G chord, which is accessed by simply adding fret 2 on string 4 and fret 1 on string 2. If you fret the G chord with your third finger on string 6 and your pinky on string 1, your middle and ring fingers are free to make this ornamentation. This riff, in the style of Don McLean, demonstrates one such possibility with this idea. The plucking-hand thumb alternates between strings 6 and 4 here throughout, while the *i*, *m*, and *a* fingers remain planted on strings 3–1, respectively.

FINGERPICKING RIFF 2 ▶ • 10:44

Similarly, the open C and Am chords are often varied to create interesting harmonies with Travis-picking patterns—something the band Kansas famously did in one of their biggest hits. In this riff, we're applying a Travis-picking pattern, which includes some pinching, to C and Am chords, but we're altering the notes on string 2 to create several different interesting chords along the way. We're also employing a pull-off at the midpoint of measures 2 and 4 for a bit of ornamentation.

FINGERPICKING RIFF 3 ▶ • 11:24

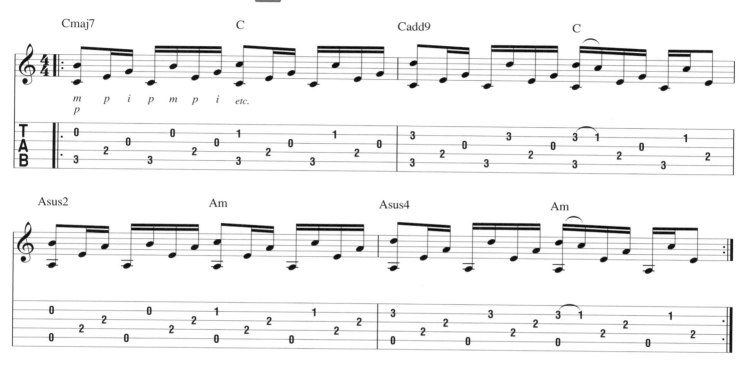

CHAPTER 6
THE SOLO ARRANGEMENTS

Congratulations on making it thus far! You've now got a good foothold on the most commonly used fingerpicking techniques, and we're about to put them to use with some introductory solo arrangements. We'll start pretty barebones here and begin to flesh things out in some of the later arrangements. There will likely still be a few awkward moves here and there that you'll need to practice a bit, but for the most part, the work you did in Chapters 1–5 prepared you well for the challenges in this chapter, as well as in Chapter 7.

AMAZING GRACE

Aside from simply playing the melody alone, the leanest arrangement we can play consists of nothing but bass notes and melody notes, so we'll start there. In this instance, the bass will almost always be played by the thumb, and the melody with the fingers. We'll play "Amazing Grace" in the key of C, as the melody will lay out nicely in open position in that key. The bass will mostly consist of dotted half notes, but we'll fill in the gaps in a few spots with some walking lines. In the second verse, we'll step it up a bit with a few more notes in the bass. Watch out for measure 26! You'll need to pay attention to the fret-hand fingering there, or you'll get tied up. Also notice the low F note in the bass in measures 19 and 27. You can either barre fret 1 at this point or use your fret-hand thumb to grab the low F.

 • 0:43

AMAZING GRACE

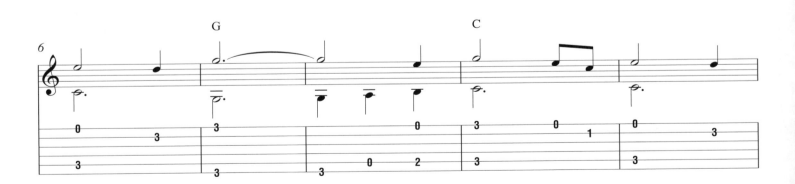

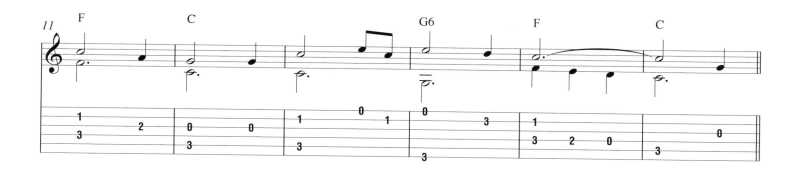

*T = Thumb on 6th string.

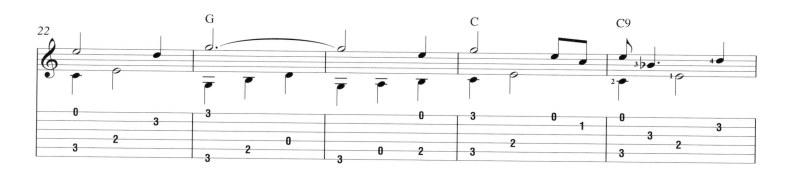

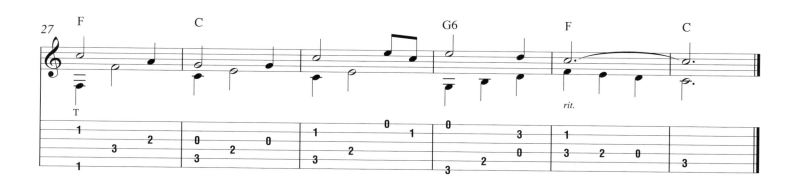

AULD LANG SYNE

We'll look at two different options for "Auld Lang Syne," both in the key of C (like "Amazing Grace"). The first option is a relatively simple block-chord arrangement, which fits its plodding, stately feel nicely. For the most part, we're just playing a chord with the melody note on top on the first beat of each measure, although there are a few spots where we add a chord on beat 3 as well. Notice the first-inversion G/B chords used throughout. This was an artistic choice I made in order to have the 3rd (the note B) in the G chord, although you could play a G note in the bass (string 6, fret 3) as well, and it would sound fine. Also notice that, for the F chords in measures 4 and 12, we play only a three-note, open-voiced F major triad in order to avoid an awkward fingering.

*T = Thumb on 6th string.

Next is a Travis-picking variation on "Auld Lang Syne." For the most part, the plucking hand patterns shouldn't pose too much of a problem. The idea is to simply keep the eighth-note pattern going as normal, but interrupt it or add pinching as necessary to play the melody notes. Although the *i*, *m*, and *a* fingers are normally assigned to strings 3–1, respectively, there are a few spots where we shift to a different string set. At those points, such as in measures 3 and 7, I've included plucking-hand fingerings. Note that we maintain the alternating bass throughout the entire arrangement, with one exception: the F chord that occurs in measure 7 and again in measure 15. At this point, the melody note dips down to the third string, so the thumb remains on string 6 for beats 3 and 4.

AULD LANG SYNE 2

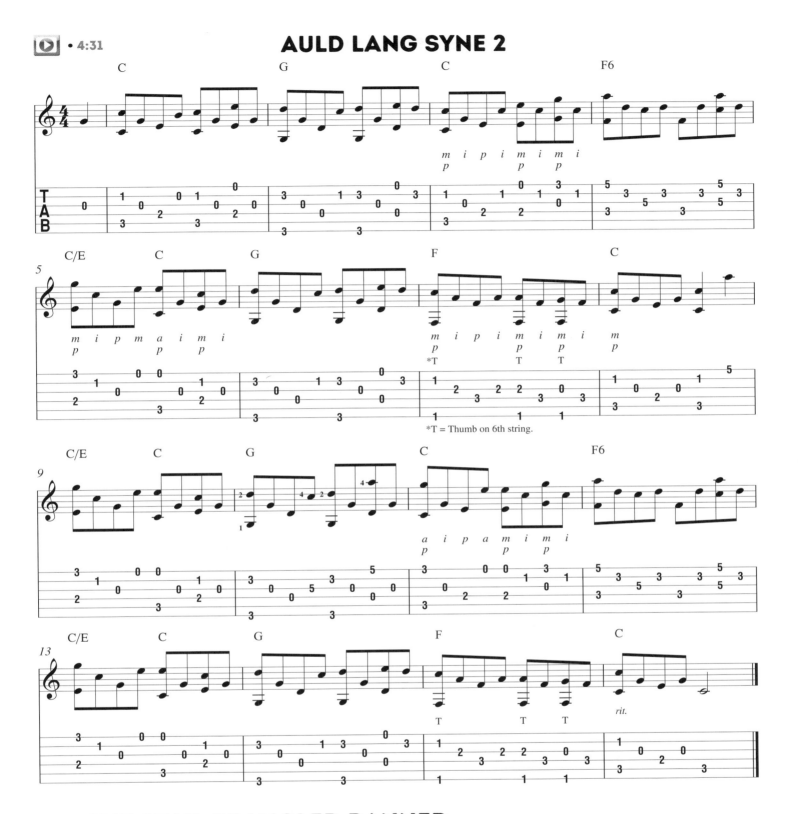

*T = Thumb on 6th string.

THE STAR-SPANGLED BANNER

Next, let's take a look at the National Anthem. For this arrangement, we're going to use a strict *contrapuntal* style with only two voices: bass and treble. We'll be using many inversions in the chords so that we're able to clearly hear the harmony throughout. The most difficult aspect of arranging this song is the range of the melody: a full octave and a half. This means that, regardless of the key we choose, we're going to have to get out of open position at some point if we want to play anything other than the melody.

Regarding the plucking hand, the concept is pretty simple: use *p* for the downstemmed notes and one of the fingers for the upstemmed notes. I prefer to alternate fingers when playing eighth notes, although at this tempo, it's not critical. There are a few spots that can be tricky for the fret hand, so watch the video to see my take on it if you're having trouble.

STAR-SPANGLED BANNER

ODE TO JOY

Classical pieces are a lot of fun to arrange on guitar because there are so many possibilities. With "Ode to Joy," you'll get plenty of practice with the pinching technique. This is the type of technique that Paul McCartney used when crafting his Beatles classic "Blackbird," which is also in the key of G. This arrangement shouldn't be too difficult, but you may want to look ahead for any fret-hand issues that could give you trouble. The video will demonstrate my preferred fingerings in this regard, but feel free to make an adjustment if something else feels more comfortable to you. Regarding the plucking hand, the vast majority of the time, I'm pinching with *p* and *m* and adding the in-between notes with *i*. This means that you'll be shifting to different string sets a good bit here and there. This arrangement is excellent practice in this regard.

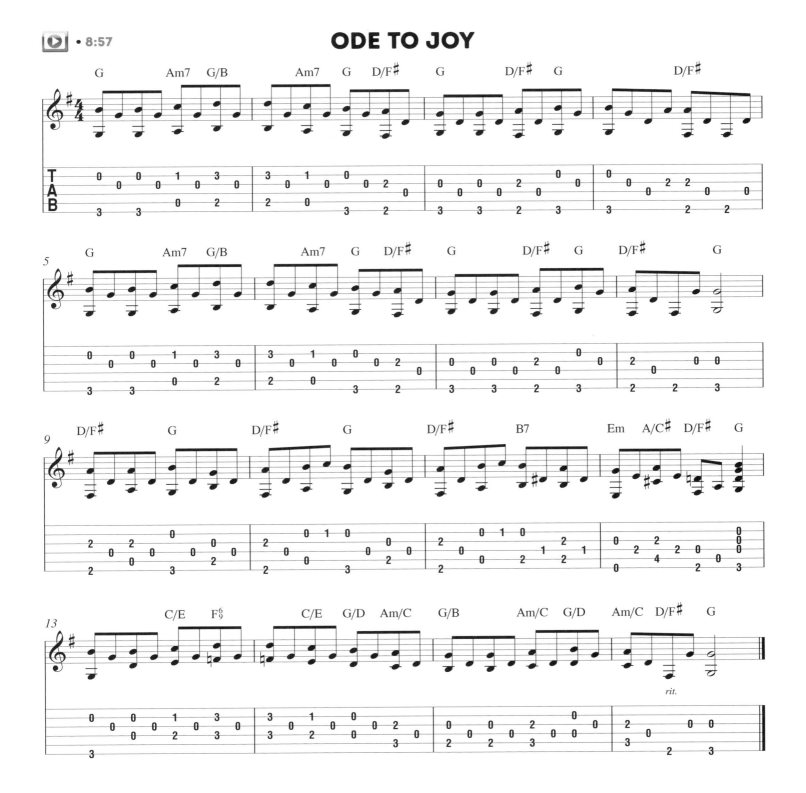

YANKEE DOODLE

Here's a fun little arrangement of "Yankee Doodle" that's divided into two distinct parts. It opens with a bouncy statement of the "A" theme, which mostly consists of triads on strings 1–3. You'll get a real workout with your inversion shapes here. Regarding the plucking hand, you can use the *i*, *m*, and *a* fingers or use a *p–i–m* combination. Both work equally well, so it's just a matter of taste.

For the "B" theme, we break into a Chet Atkins-style Travis-picking approach and a shuffle feel. A few things are of note here: notice that we play only quarter notes on beat 4 of every measure, breaking the constant eighth-note pulse. This is something I like to do occasionally to provide more of a bouncy feel. Also be sure to notice in the reprise, starting in measure 17, the syncopation is slightly different in the melody. For the D chords, I'm using a half barre at fret 2 with my index finger and then hinging it on beat 4 to access the open E string. In other words, I keep it pressed down to string 3 but angle the finger so that it lifts off string 1. Check out the video to see this in action.

 • 10:38

YANKEE DOODLE

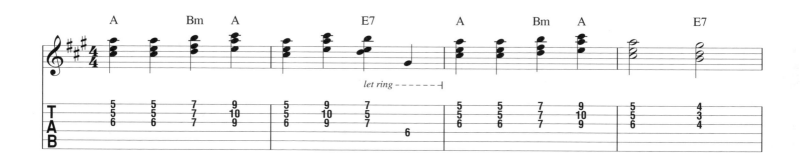

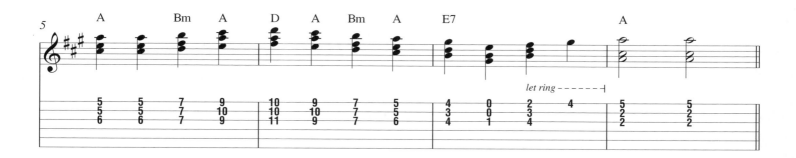

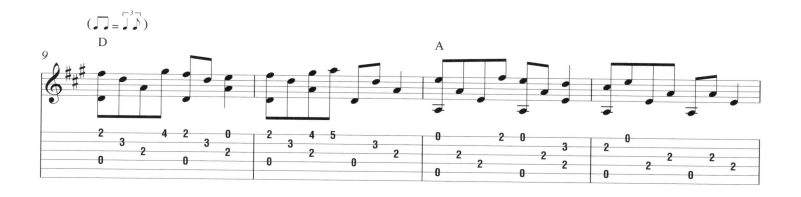

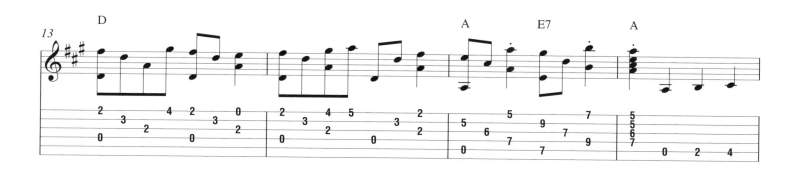

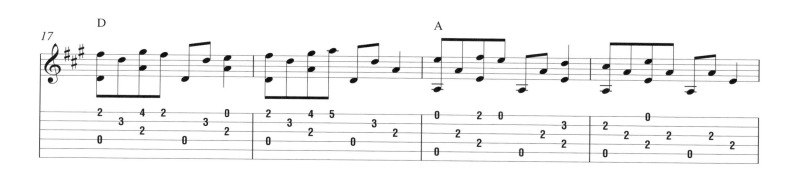

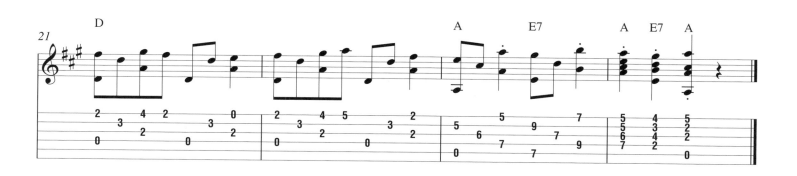

AMERICA THE BEAUTIFUL

This arrangement of "America the Beautiful" in the key of A is the most advanced Travis-picking example in the book thus far. The patterns aren't anything out of the ordinary, in general, but there are several spots where we're using specific voicings to facilitate the range of the melody. The G♯ at fret 4, string 1 in measure 3 is a bit of a reach but shouldn't pose a serious problem for most people (I've added fret-hand fingerings in the tricky spots). Regarding the plucking hand, the thumb plays, almost without exception, the lowest notes on beats 1 and 3 throughout the entire piece. The notes on top can be handled with the fingers, using whichever method feels most comfortable for you.

AMERICA THE BEAUTIFUL

• 12:27

GREENSLEEVES

A popular song dating back centuries, "Greensleeves" contains a captivating melody that's been arranged for many instruments over the years. This arrangement, like some of the others, is split into two distinct parts. The first presentation of the melody, in A minor, is a fairly plain-stated reading in block-chord style. This shouldn't prove too difficult, as most of the chord forms are readily accessible in open position, and the demands on the plucking hand are minimal. Watch out for measure 7, however, where you'll need to make a bit of a stretch on the E chord for the F♯ melody note at fret 4, string 4.

In measure 16, at the end of the first statement, we have a surprise A7, which we soon discover sets up the next section, which modulates to D minor. For this part, we use a more intricate arpeggio pattern that's somewhat of a mutated Travis-picking style that's been varied to fit the 6/8 time signature. The basic eighth-note pattern here is thumb/finger–finger–thumb/finger, as evidenced in the first half of measure 17. Occasionally, a 16th note that fits in between the notes of the basic pattern appears in the melody. Your plucking hand will shift between two basic positions in this section: 1) *p* on strings 4 and 3, *i* on string 2, and *m* on string 1, and 2) *p* on strings 5 and 4, and *i*, *m*, and *a* on strings 3–1, respectively. However, there are a few exceptions to this, as seen in measure 19, where *p* remains on string 4, and *i*, *m*, and *a* are on strings 1–3. I've included plucking-hand fingerings for most of this section. The other tricky part of this section is that you'll need to shift out of open position a few times. You don't stay long, though, so it shouldn't be too taxing.

▶ • 14:01

GREENSLEEVES

CHAPTER 7
CREATING YOUR OWN ARRANGEMENTS

There's little more satisfying than coming up with your own great-sounding arrangements of your favorite songs. It's a fantastic learning process, incredibly fulfilling, and you glow with pride as you tell your friends and family that it's your own unique arrangement. Some songs certainly lend themselves to solo-guitar arrangement better than others, and we'll discover some of the reasons for that in this chapter. But there are plenty of fish in the sea, and you're not going to run out of options anytime soon, I assure you.

IT STARTS WITH THE MELODY

When selecting a song for solo guitar, it starts with the melody. More melodic songs tend to make nicer arrangements because there aren't any lyrics to provide another source of interest. While songs like "Brick House" have their own appeal when performed by a full band with vocals, they tend to lose their interest as solo arrangements. Therefore, you'll likely want a song in which the melody has a nice bit of motion in it. Some of the old jazz standards, such as "All of Me," "Fly Me to the Moon," and "Unforgettable," are excellent in this regard, as are some classical pieces, but there are plenty of more modern songs, such as "The Long and Winding Road" (The Beatles) and "Viva La Vida" (Coldplay), that fit the bill as well if those don't appeal to you.

In addition to the melody, there are other concerns to think about as well. Let's look at each.

RANGE

This is a pretty important one, because the guitar isn't a piano. By that I mean that we don't have the almost limitless range that a piano does. So, if you pick a melody that's all over the place, it may prove difficult, depending on the key. We have a couple of options in that regard:

- **Transposition:** Just because the original song appears in a certain key doesn't mean we have to keep it there. In fact, it's incredibly common for a singer to change the key when covering another artist's song, and we can do the same on guitar. "Open-string keys" (C, G, E, A, etc.) tend to work well on the guitar because of the extra possibilities they afford.

- **Octave transference:** Another option is to transpose a part of the melody up or down an octave. It's usually best to do this at the start of a new section—or at least at the beginning of a line—so the original contour can at least be maintained at the micro level.

RHYTHMIC COMPLEXITY

Another concern is how rhythmically complex the melody is. If it contains a lot of 16th notes that can't really be pared down, for example, it might be best to look for another song. That's not to say that it can't be done, of course, but it will likely require some more advanced arranging techniques that will take a bit more skill to work up. If you're just starting out with arranging, I'd recommend melodies that contain longer, more sustained notes.

BLUES INFLECTIONS

Another thing to consider is how well the melody can be represented on the guitar. While the guitar is certainly capable of emulating blues vocal inflections, it may prove more difficult to do that if you also have to play bass notes and/or chords simultaneously. Therefore, it's best to initially avoid songs with a lot of "in the cracks" notes, as they're likely to prove a bit problematic to the novice arranger.

ADDING THE BASS

After deciding on a melody, I like to proceed with finding a good bass-line foundation. In other words, finding where on the fretboard you'll be playing most of the root notes of the chords (if you add them) that accompany the melody. Should you play the F bass note on fret 3 of string 4 or down on fret 1 of string 6? Issues like this may also be a determining factor (along with the melody) in choosing the key of the arrangement. It may also result in choosing to use drop D tuning, for example.

When you decide on a texture for the arrangement (see below), it will also help to define the rhythmic role of the bass (i.e., whether it will predominantly play half notes, quarter notes, etc.).

FLESHING IT OUT

Once you have the melody and bass more or less configured, you can decide how you'd like the texture to be fleshed out. Will it sound best with arpeggios, block chords, or Travis picking? Or maybe it will be a hybrid of two techniques. This is where you get to be creative with your arrangement, because every melody will present its own unique challenges and possibilities. The feel of the original song can help you decide in this regard. For example, if the song has a constant, busy, bouncing rhythm, then a Travis-picking approach can help to mimic that. If it's a slow, wistful ballad, perhaps block-chord style or arpeggios (or a combination of the two) would be best.

REHARMONIZATION: THE ARRANGER'S SECRET WEAPON

One of my favorite things to do with an arrangement is to try to place my own little spin on the song. This can sometimes be done by changing the rhythmic feel—perhaps playing a song with a shuffle feel instead of a straight feel—or drastically changing the tempo, etc. Another, often more subtle way of doing this is by reharmonizing the melody with different chords than those used in the original. Generally speaking, you want to avoid chords that would clash with the notes of the melody. So, for example, if the melody notes are C and E, you probably wouldn't want to play an A chord or a C♯m chord because they contain C♯, which would directly clash with C. But there are plenty of other options available. The better your harmonic vocabulary, the more options you'll have at your disposal, but even "hunting and pecking" can be fun if you're not terribly chord-savvy. For example, try various bass notes under the melody to see if something catches your ear. It doesn't have to be drastic to make a nice, little impact. We'll make use of this concept in our full arrangement later this chapter.

There's no rule that says you have to adhere to one technique throughout the whole song, either. It could be that, in the chorus, the melody moves into a range that lends itself more to one method or the other. Or perhaps the original version of the song changes significantly in feel during one section; you can use different techniques to help convey that change (e.g., moving from Travis picking to block chords). Again, every melody will be different, and you'll need to spend a bit of time with it, perhaps trying out a few ideas before something works. If you're patient, however, the solution will usually present itself and the arrangement will begin to take shape.

SAMPLE ARRANGEMENT CREATION: IT CAME UPON A MIDNIGHT CLEAR

Well, that's enough blabbing; let's check out how some of this advice can help build an arrangement from the ground up. Along with jazz standards and classical pieces, Christmas songs are usually ripe for the picking in terms of solo arrangements. We'll work with the classic "It Came Upon a Midnight Clear" for this example.

MELODY

The first arrangement of this song that I found had the melody in the key of G, and it spanned from B to B—exactly one octave. Generally speaking, for a beginning arrangement, if I can fit the melody notes entirely within strings 1–3 in first position, I prefer to do that because it leaves the D string open for notes below the melody. In order to do that here, though, I'd have to either arrange the song in the key of E♭ (in which case, the lowest note would be the open G string) or the key of E (in which case, G♯ [fret 1, string 3] would be the lowest note). The key of E♭ is not preferable for a beginning guitar arrangement, so I examined the key of E. Here's what the melody would look like in the key of E:

• 3:22

IT CAME UPON A MIDNIGHT CLEAR
(MELODY IN THE KEY OF E)

So, as you can see, the melody is easily playable in open position and lays out fairly nicely. However, when I started to add bass and chords to it, I encountered a few awkward spots that made me think there would be a better option. Since the lowest note of the melody only occurs for a few beats, I decided to just put the song in the key of C and take advantage of the comfortable forms in open position there. The lowest note then becomes E at fret 2 of string 4, but since it's so brief, it's not a deal-breaker. So here's the melody now in the key of C:

IT CAME UPON A MIDNIGHT CLEAR
(MELODY IN THE KEY OF C)

ADDING THE BASS

With the melody set, it's time to add some bass. As a starting point, I'd suggest using the bass and chords that are present in the most common version of the song. Hal Leonard publishes many excellent Christmas songbooks that can be used for this. Once you have a standard version down, you can begin to experiment with other harmony options if you'd like.

▶ · 6:24 IT CAME UPON A MIDNIGHT CLEAR
(BASS NOTES ADDED)

FLESHING IT OUT

Finally, we need to decide on a texture. Since the song is in 3/4, standard Travis picking is out because it requires an even number of beats per measure. And because I wanted the arrangement to have a flowing quality, I decided against block chords because I thought they would sound a little too plodding. So I settled on an arpeggiation approach, filling in the gaps when necessary to keep something happening on just about every beat. Between the melody and the bass line, there really wasn't a lot more needed to flesh it out, but I added a few eighth notes here and there to keep it interesting.

Throughout the arrangement, play the downstemmed notes with the thumb and upstemmed notes with the fingers. You'll spend the vast majority of the time with your fingers on strings 3–1, but you will need to creep down to string 4 in measures 17–18, 22, and 31–32. Notice the reharmonization in measures 28–29, which helps provide a nice little twist at the end. I've added some suggested fret-hand fingerings for measures 17–20, which can get a little tricky.

 • 7:41

IT CAME UPON A MIDNIGHT CLEAR
(FULL ARRANGEMENT)

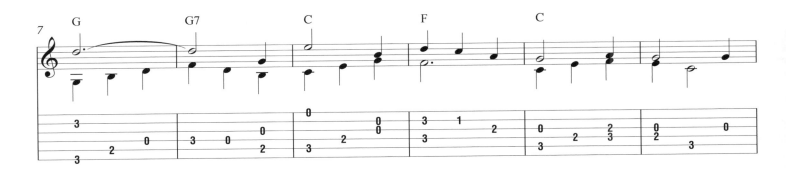

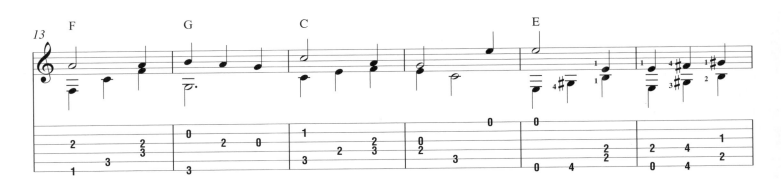

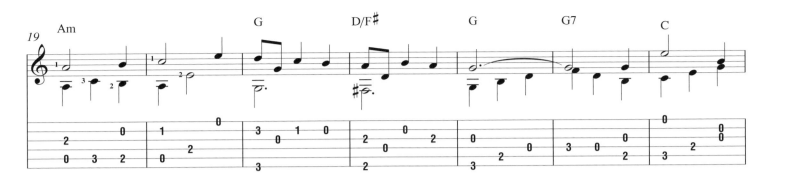

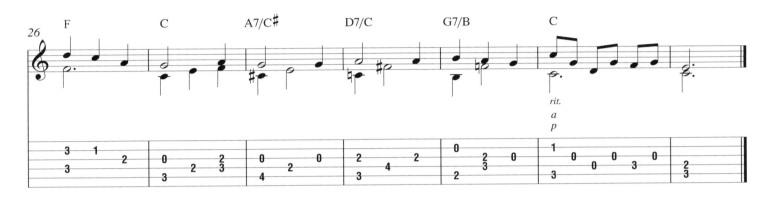

AFTERWORD

That brings us to the end of the book. By this point, you should possess a good grasp on many useful fingerpicking techniques and a working knowledge of how to start creating your very own arrangements. What makes it always interesting is that each and every song is different. There will always be new challenges with every one, and it will always be rewarding when you discover the solutions to those challenges. I encourage you to learn many other arrangements while creating your own, as each person's take on a song will most likely teach you something. Hal Leonard has numerous books in this regard, including *Fingerpicking Acoustic*, *Fingerpicking Blues*, *Fingerpicking Pop*, *Fingerpicking Standards*, and many more that would provide a wealth of material with which to continue honing your skills. As with anything, the more you work on it, the more it will become second nature. Before you know it, you'll be thinking of how you can arrange a song before you even pick up your guitar. Best of luck to you, and keep on pickin'!

FINGERPICKING GUITAR BOOKS

Hone your fingerpicking skills with these great songbooks featuring solo guitar arrangements in standard notation and tablature. The arrangements in these books are carefully written for intermediate-level guitarists. Each song combines melody and harmony in one superb guitar fingerpicking arrangement. Each book also includes an introduction to basic fingerstyle guitar.

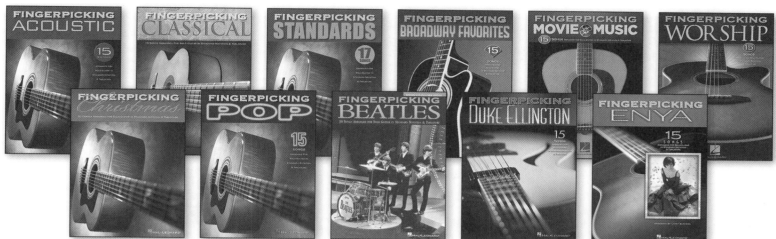

FINGERPICKING ACOUSTIC
00699614...$12.99

FINGERPICKING ACOUSTIC ROCK
00699764...$12.99

FINGERPICKING BACH
00699793...$10.99

FINGERPICKING BALLADS
00699717...$9.99

FINGERPICKING BEATLES
00699049...$19.99

FINGERPICKING BEETHOVEN
00702390...$7.99

FINGERPICKING BLUES
00701277 ....$7.99

FINGERPICKING BROADWAY FAVORITES
00699843...$9.99

FINGERPICKING BROADWAY HITS
00699838...$7.99

FINGERPICKING CELTIC FOLK
00701148...$10.99

FINGERPICKING CHILDREN'S SONGS
00699712...$9.99

FINGERPICKING CHRISTIAN
00701076 ....$7.99

FINGERPICKING CHRISTMAS
00699599...$9.99

FINGERPICKING CHRISTMAS CLASSICS
00701695...$7.99

FINGERPICKING CHRISTMAS SONGS
00171333...$9.99

FINGERPICKING CLASSICAL
00699620...$8.95

FINGERPICKING COUNTRY
00699687...$10.99

FINGERPICKING DISNEY
00699711...$12.99

FINGERPICKING DUKE ELLINGTON
00699845...$9.99

FINGERPICKING ENYA
00701161...$9.99

FINGERPICKING GOSPEL
00701059...$7.99

FINGERPICKING GUITAR BIBLE
00691040 ....$19.99

FINGERPICKING HIT SONGS
00160195...$12.99

FINGERPICKING HYMNS
00699688...$8.95

FINGERPICKING IRISH SONGS
00701965...$7.99

FINGERPICKING JAZZ FAVORITES
00699844 ....$7.99

FINGERPICKING JAZZ STANDARDS
00699840...$7.99

FINGERPICKING LATIN FAVORITES
00699842...$9.99

FINGERPICKING LATIN STANDARDS
00699837...$10.99

FINGERPICKING ANDREW LLOYD WEBBER
00699839...$12.99

FINGERPICKING LOVE SONGS
00699841...$10.99

FINGERPICKING LOVE STANDARDS
00699836 ....$9.99

FINGERPICKING LULLABYES
00701276...$9.99

FINGERPICKING MOVIE MUSIC
00699919...$9.99

FINGERPICKING MOZART
00699794...$8.95

FINGERPICKING POP
00699615...$9.99

FINGERPICKING POPULAR HITS
00139079...$12.99

FINGERPICKING PRAISE
00699714...$9.99

FINGERPICKING ROCK
00699716...$10.99

FINGERPICKING STANDARDS
00699613...$12.99

FINGERPICKING WEDDING
00699637...$9.99

FINGERPICKING WORSHIP
00700554...$9.99

FINGERPICKING NEIL YOUNG – GREATEST HITS
00700134...$12.99

FINGERPICKING YULETIDE
00699654...$9.99

HAL•LEONARD®

7777 W. BLUEMOUND RD. P.O. BOX 13819
MILWAUKEE, WISCONSIN 53213

Visit Hal Leonard online at **www.halleonard.com**

Prices, contents and availability subject to change without notice.

Get Better at Guitar

...with these Great Guitar Instruction Books from Hal Leonard!

101 GUITAR TIPS
STUFF ALL THE PROS KNOW AND USE
by Adam St. James

This book contains invaluable guidance on everything from scales and music theory to truss rod adjustments, proper recording studio set-ups, and much more. The book also features snippets of advice from some of the most celebrated guitarists and producers in the music business, including B.B. King, Steve Vai, Joe Satriani, Warren Haynes, Laurence Juber, Pete Anderson, Tom Dowd and others, culled from the author's hundreds of interviews.

00695737 Book/Online Audio $16.99

AMAZING PHRASING
50 WAYS TO IMPROVE YOUR IMPROVISATIONAL SKILLS
by Tom Kolb

This book/CD pack explores all the main components necessary for crafting well-balanced rhythmic and melodic phrases. It also explains how these phrases are put together to form cohesive solos. Many styles are covered – rock, blues, jazz, fusion, country, Latin, funk and more – and all of the concepts are backed up with musical examples. The companion CD contains 89 demos for listening, and most tracks feature full-band backing.

00695583 Book/CD Pack...$19.95

BLUES YOU CAN USE – 2ND EDITION
by John Ganapes

This comprehensive source for learning blues guitar is designed to develop both your lead and rhythm playing. Includes: 21 complete solos • blues chords, progressions and riffs • turnarounds • movable scales and soloing techniques • string bending • utilizing the entire fingerboard • and more. This second edition now includes audio and video access online!

00142420 Book/Online Media..................................$19.99

FRETBOARD MASTERY
by Troy Stetina

Untangle the mysterious regions of the guitar fretboard and unlock your potential. *Fretboard Mastery* familiarizes you with all the shapes you need to know by applying them in real musical examples, thereby reinforcing and reaffirming your newfound knowledge. The result is a much higher level of comprehension and retention.

00695331 Book/Online Audio $19.99

FRETBOARD ROADMAPS – 2ND EDITION
ESSENTIAL GUITAR PATTERNS THAT ALL THE PROS KNOW AND USE
by Fred Sokolow

The updated edition of this bestseller features more songs, updated lessons, and a full audio CD! Learn to play lead and rhythm anywhere on the fretboard, in any key; play a variety of lead guitar styles; play chords and progressions anywhere on the fretboard; expand your chord vocabulary; and learn to think musically – the way the pros do.

00695941 Book/CD Pack..$14.95

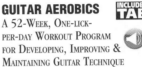

GUITAR AEROBICS
A 52-WEEK, ONE-LICK-PER-DAY WORKOUT PROGRAM FOR DEVELOPING, IMPROVING & MAINTAINING GUITAR TECHNIQUE
by Troy Nelson

From the former editor of *Guitar One* magazine, here is a daily dose of vitamins to keep your chops fine tuned! Musical styles include rock, blues, jazz, metal, country, and funk. Techniques taught include alternate picking, arpeggios, sweep picking, string skipping, legato, string bending, and rhythm guitar. These exercises will increase speed, and improve dexterity and pick- and fret-hand accuracy. The accompanying audio includes all 365 workout licks plus play-along grooves in every style at eight different metronome settings.

00695946 Book/Online Audio $19.99

GUITAR CLUES
OPERATION PENTATONIC
by Greg Koch

Join renowned guitar master Greg Koch as he clues you in to a wide variety of fun and valuable pentatonic scale applications. Whether you're new to improvising or have been doing it for a while, this book/CD pack will provide loads of delicious licks and tricks that you can use right away, from volume swells and chicken pickin' to intervallic and chordal ideas. The CD includes 65 demo and play-along tracks.

00695827 Book/CD Pack...$19.95

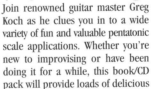

INTRODUCTION TO GUITAR TONE & EFFECTS
by David M. Brewster

This book/CD pack teaches the basics of guitar tones and effects, with audio examples on CD. Readers will learn about: overdrive, distortion and fuzz • using equalizers • modulation effects • reverb and delay • multi-effect processors • and more.

00695766 Book/CD Pack..$14.99

PICTURE CHORD ENCYCLOPEDIA

This comprehensive guitar chord resource for all playing styles and levels features five voicings of 44 chord qualities for all twelve keys – 2,640 chords in all! For each, there is a clearly illustrated chord frame, as well as *an actual photo* of the chord being played! Includes info on basic fingering principles, open chords and barre chords, partial chords and broken-set forms, and more.

00695224..$19.95

SCALE CHORD RELATIONSHIPS
by Michael Mueller & Jeff Schroedl

This book teaches players how to determine which scales to play with which chords, so guitarists will never have to fear chord changes again! This book/audio pack explains how to: recognize keys • analyze chord progressions • use the modes • play over nondiatonic harmony • use harmonic and melodic minor scales • use symmetrical scales such as chromatic, whole-tone and diminished scales • incorporate exotic scales such as Hungarian major and Gypsy minor • and much more!

00695563 Book/Online Audio $14.99

SPEED MECHANICS FOR LEAD GUITAR

Take your playing to the stratosphere with the most advanced lead book by this proven heavy metal author. *Speed Mechanics* is the ultimate technique book for developing the kind of speed and precision in today's explosive playing styles. Learn the fastest ways to achieve speed and control, secrets to make your practice time really count, and how to open your ears and make your musical ideas more solid and tangible. Packed with over 200 vicious exercises including Troy's scorching version of "Flight of the Bumblebee." Music and examples demonstrated on CD. 89-minute audio.

00699323 Book/CD Pack..$19.95

TOTAL ROCK GUITAR
A COMPLETE GUIDE TO LEARNING ROCK GUITAR
by Troy Stetina

This unique and comprehensive source for learning rock guitar is designed to develop both lead and rhythm playing. It covers: getting a tone that rocks • open chords, power chords and barre chords • riffs, scales and licks • string bending, strumming, palm muting, harmonics and alternate picking • all rock styles • and much more. The examples are in standard notation with chord grids and tab, and the audio includes full-band backing for all 22 songs.

00695246 Book/Online Audio $19.99